THE SECRET OF
CHRIST OUR
LIFE

THE SECRET OF
CHRIST OUR LIFE

Andrew Murray

CLC PUBLICATIONS

Fort Washington, PA 19034

The Secret of Christ Our Life
Published by CLC Publications

U.S.A.
P.O. Box 1449, Fort Washington, PA 19034

UNITED KINGDOM
CLC International (UK)
Unit 5, Glendale Avenue, Sandycroft, Flintshire, CH5 2QP

Printed in the United States of America

ISBN (paperback): 978-1-61958-282-8
ISBN (e-book): 978-1-61958-283-5

Italics in Scripture quotations are the emphasis of the author.

Cover design by Mitch Bolton.

PREFACE

FROM St. Paul's glorious confession of faith in Galatians 2:20, I would emphasize especially the words *for me* and *in me*. Here lies the twofold secret of the Christian life. About the first he says, "I live by faith in the Son of God, who loved me and gave Himself *for me*." About the other he says, "It is no longer I who live, but Christ lives *in me*." The first, *for me*, points to the immovable foundation of our hope. Christ was made sin for us, bearing our sin. The second, *in me*, points to the life-power in us, whereby Christ dwelling in us works out our salvation day by day.

Most Christians get no farther than *for me*. They attempt to live for Christ in the strength of that word, but they fail. In these words, *for me*, lie the roots of the tree of life, but more is needed before there can be fruit. There must be a stem and branches, and we do not have these before Christ actually dwells in our hearts by faith and is our life.

We find this in our Lord's words on that last night when He spoke of our abiding in *Him* and He in *us*. This was to be the revelation of Christ in our hearts by the power of the Holy Spirit. "At that day you will know that I am in My Father, and you in Me, and I in you" (John 14:20). Then He promises that He will reveal Himself to us by the Spirit, and that He and the Father will make Their dwelling in us. In St. John's Gospel, chapter 15, it is recorded that He repeatedly said, "Abide in Me, and I in you" (15:4); "I am the vine, you are the branches. He who abides in Me, and I in him, bears much fruit" (15:5).

These words teach us that the branches remain in the vine and the vine ever supplies sap and life-power to the branches. So our faith must ever be in Christ as crucified *for us* that He Himself may abide *in us* as our life.

A poor spiritual life results when a Christian thinks, "Christ for me" is enough, and does not know or even desire "Christ in me." This is what Christ actually promises. His love desires an intimate, unbroken fellowship with Himself. It is only by His abiding in us that we shall bear "much fruit" to the glory of the Father.

It is with the desire to help God's children who long to know all that Christ can be *for* and *in* them that I have sought grace from God to make clear in this booklet the meaning of the words, "*Christ our life*." The message I bring is a glorious one, namely this, that as the Son of God led a human life in the days of His flesh, He now desires to continue His life in every redeemed soul, every member of the body of which He is the Head. Oh, that we would daily give Christ the opportunity of showing that He lives in us and is Himself responsible that we are enabled to do God's will!

May God the Father teach us by His Spirit daily, in the quiet hour, to commune with our Lord Jesus so that with St. Paul we may say, "It is no longer I who live, but Christ lives in me."

ANDREW MURRAY

God's Plan of Salvation

When Christ who is our life appears, then you also will appear with Him in glory.

Colossians 3:4

AFTER Adam had sinned and brought death upon himself and his descendants, God gave the promise that a man born of woman should conquer the power of Satan and sin. This Man, who was the Son of God, the Bible calls the second Adam. For, concerning our human progenitor, we read: "Adam, who is a type of Him who was to come" (Rom. 5:14). Thus the second Adam was in every respect to be analogous to the first.

Adam not only brought the curse of sin and death upon his descendants but actually bequeathed to them a life which was the cause of their being wholly dominated by evil. In this way, the old sinful nature of Adam survived in his descendants. The old nature lived in them and held sway. Likewise, Christ by His death not only delivered us from the power of sin and death but He Himself lives in each of His redeemed ones and is their life.

We are too apt to think of Christ as in heaven, and from there living for and through us; but the last night He was on earth He taught that as His Father lived and worked in Him here on earth, even so would He dwell in us and work in us.

The full gospel is contained in these words: "[Christ] is our life"; "Christ lives in me" (Gal. 2:20); "Do you not know yourselves, that Jesus Christ is in you?" (2 Cor. 13:5).

Many Christians forget this. They believe Christ died on the cross for them, and lives in heaven for them, but hardly that Christ is *in* them. The powerlessness of the church is mainly due to this. *We do not realize that the almighty Christ dwells in us.* We must know and experience and testify to this great truth if there is to be a real and lasting revival in the church of Christ. Then we shall know what it means to give ourselves wholly to Christ, always to abide in fellowship with Him, that His work may be accomplished through us. "Christ lives in me" (Gal. 2:20); "For to me, to live is Christ" (Phil. 1:21).

The Twofold Life

I have come that they may have life, and that they may have it more abundantly.

John 10:10

EVERYONE can understand the difference between life that is weak and sickly and life that has abundant vitality. Thus St. Paul speaks of the Christian life of the Corinthians as not spiritual but carnal, as of young children in Christ incapable of assimilating strong meat or of understanding the deeper truths of the gospel (see 1 Corinthians 3 and Hebrews 5). There are some, the majority of Christians, who never advance beyond first principles. They are dull of hearing and remain carnal Christians. There are others again, a minority, who indeed show forth the abundant riches of grace. All through the history of the church we find this difference. In our day, too, the number is small of those who seek to live wholly for God and, being spiritually minded, have large thoughts of the abundant life there is in Christ. These few witness to the glory of Christ as "full of grace and truth" (John 1:14); "And of His fullness we have all received, and grace for grace" (1:16).

The preacher's aim should be so to declare the fullness of God's grace in Jesus Christ as to make Christians ashamed of the poverty of their spiritual life, and to encourage them to believe that "life abundant" in the fullness of the Spirit is for them.

Dear reader, ask yourself if you are living such an abundant life as Jesus came to bestow. Is it manifest in your love to the Savior and in the abundant fruit you bear to the glory of God in soul-winning?—for remember, "he who wins souls is wise" (Prov. 11:30). If not, pray God to strengthen your faith so that He will be able to make all grace abound toward you that you, *always* having *all* sufficiency, may *abound* in every good work. Let Jesus be precious to you and daily communion with Him indispensable. He will teach you by His Holy Spirit to honor Him by an abundant life.

Life Abundant

Where sin abounded, grace abounded much more, so that as sin reigned in death, even so grace might reign through righteousness to eternal life through Jesus Christ our Lord.

Romans 5:20–21

HOW little this truth is grasped or understood. That sin abounds we know full well. But do we believe that "grace abounds more exceedingly " and enables us to reign over sin? Yet it is absolutely necessary that we grasp this truth if we would have life abundant in Christ. Read Second Corinthians 9:8 and observe the words *all* and *every*, denoting abundance. "God is able to make *all grace* abound toward you, that you, *always* (without exception) having *all* sufficiency in *all* things (every possible need), may have an abundance for *every* good work." Dear reader, say to yourself: "Is this abundant all-abounding life for me? Truly, if God is faithful it is possible for me! Oh God, write this truth upon my heart!"

Now take St. Paul's prayer in Colossians 1:9–11, so that you may be able to pray it first for yourself and then for others—"[We] do not cease to pray for you, and to ask that you may be filled with the knowledge of His will in *all* wisdom and spiritual understanding; that you may walk worthy of the Lord, *fully* pleasing Him, being fruitful in *every* good work and increasing in the knowledge of God; strengthened with *all* might, according to His glorious power, for *all* patience and longsuffering with joy."

(See also 1 John 3:22.) These words of the Holy Spirit are almost beyond our grasp. Let us continually take them to God that He Himself through His Holy Spirit may make them to live in our hearts. By them we shall attain to a firm and joyous faith. With such a *God*, with such abounding *grace*—much more abundant than the easily besetting sin—with such a *Lord Jesus* to give grace and cause grace to reign—thank God, I may believe that life abundant is for me!

Christ Lives in Me

*I have been crucified with Christ; it is no longer I who live,
but Christ lives in me.*

IN these words St. Paul expresses three great thoughts:
First, "I have been crucified with Christ." When
Christ died on the cross He identified all God's people
with Himself in that death. As we all died in Adam and
have inherited Adam's sinful nature, so we all have been
crucified with Christ; and the power of His death works
in us daily in order that, having died to sin in Christ, we
may live unto God. Our union with the crucified Christ
is vital and complete. The power of His death and of His
life is active in us.

St. Paul's second thought is, "It is no longer I who
live." Having actually participated in the death of Christ he
could say, "No longer do I live." My life has been yielded
to death upon the cross of Christ. By faith I see my life
under sentence of death *canceled*. It is still mine in my
flesh wherein no good thing dwells, but *I am free* in Christ
so that I no longer serve sin as long as I abide in Christ.

His third thought, "Christ lives in me," is the true
secret of a Christlike life. Christ was not only *crucified* for
me; He does not live only in heaven to *intercede* for me.
No! *Christ lives in me*. He Himself said that even as His
Father dwelt and worked in Him, even so He dwells and
works in us. He is truly the life in us by which we live.

Oh, Christian, I beseech you, take time to meditate and adore. Allow the Holy Spirit to make these words live in your heart. This is the work of the Holy Spirit: to manifest Christ in you, to glorify Him in you with the heavenly glory which fills all things. Do not imagine that Christ's life can be manifested in us unless we die to the world and to self. Christ had to die. You are crucified with Christ and must experience the crucified life. The rest will follow—"I live no longer, Christ lives in me." "Thanks be to God for His indescribable gift!" (2 Cor. 9:15).

The Life of Faith

The life which I now live in the flesh I live by faith in the
Son of God, who loved me and gave Himself for me.

Galatians 2:20

THESE words are St. Paul's reply to the objection: "If you say, 'Christ lives in me,' where does *your* will come in?" If Christ does actually live in you, and holds Himself responsible for your life, what remains for *you* to do?

St. Paul's words contain the secret of the true life of faith. Elsewhere he prays for believers, "that Christ may dwell in your hearts through faith" (Eph. 3:17). Here we see the great work that faith has to accomplish in us, and for us, moment by moment, in order to allow the living Lord to work His will in us. Christ will accomplish the words in our hearts.

Because of His divinity, it is natural for the Lord Jesus to fill all things, to be all in all, and especially—by means of the new birth—in the hearts of His children.

Christ's own words to His disciples best explain this. Even as the Father dwelt in Him and worked His work in Him, so our Lord dwells in us and works His work in us. The Son expressed the Father; we are to express *Christ*. The Father worked in the Son, and the Son worked out what the Father had wrought in Him; Christ works in us and enables us to carry on *His* work. This is His gift to us.

The only attitude that becomes us is one of trust, strengthening our faith in the assurance that "He loved me and gave Himself for me." He and I are eternally and inseparably one. "He lives in me."

This is almost too great to grasp or to believe, and yet it is God's truth. The child of God needs time for meditation and adoration so that the Spirit of God may reveal to him how completely He will fill our being, accomplishing the work in us. Oh, the depth of the riches and the wisdom and the knowledge of God! How unsearchable are His judgments, and His ways past finding out! Oh, the depth of the love of God in Christ! Let us sacrifice *all* that we may know and trust and honor His love.

Day 6

The Ever-Abiding Spirit

[The Father] will give you another Helper, that He may abide with you forever . . . He dwells with you and will be in you.

John 14:16–17

WE who have been born again usually think of the abiding presence of the Lord Jesus as the reality promised to us. Christ distinctly says, "Abide in Me, and I in you" (John 15:4); "Abide in My love" (15:9). In today's text, however, He speaks of "abiding" in relation to the indwelling and work of the *Holy Spirit*. Read the text over again and you will see that Christ abiding in us and our abiding in Him—"you in Me, and I in you" (14:20)—is altogether dependent upon the indwelling of the Holy Spirit. Therefore it is of the greatest importance that we rightly grasp the fact of the ever-abiding indwelling of the Holy Spirit.

This truth is meant to be realized each day as we appear in God's presence—by renewing and confessing of our faith in the ever-abiding indwelling of the Spirit. In His office as Comforter and Helper He was sent to compensate the disciples for the absence of Christ's physical presence, and with this heavenly help He helps us each hour. It is through Him that we have Christ in our hearts—a living, mighty force animating and enlightening us and filling our lives. This realization can be ours if we come into touch with God in Christ each day, in that way receiving fresh power to influence and bless others.

Oh my brother, begin each day with the triune God! Take time to worship God in Christ. Take time to yield yourself to the Holy Spirit and to count upon Him to accomplish a great work in you. He will do this by making Christ ever present in you.

Christ and the Spirit

"He who believes in Me, as the Scripture has said, out of his heart will flow rivers of living water." But this He spoke concerning the Spirit, whom those believing in Him would receive.

John 7:38–39

EACH Person of the blessed Trinity gives honor to the other. The Father seeks the honor of the Son and the Son seeks the honor of the Spirit, and the Spirit honors the Son. So in our text today we hear Christ calling us to *believe in Him*, confident that the Holy Spirit will work powerfully in us according to the measure of our faith in Christ. On the other hand Christ says, "[The Spirit] will not speak on His own authority, but whatever He hears He will speak . . . He will glorify Me, for He will take of what is Mine and declare it to you" (John 16:13–14).

Here we learn the important lesson that we must not expect the Holy Spirit always to give us tokens of His presence. He will ever seek to fix our attention upon Christ. The surest way to be filled with the Spirit is whole-heartedly to occupy ourselves by faith with Christ. We may rely upon the Holy Spirit to enable us to do this.

Begin every morning in God's presence and there commit yourself to Christ to accomplish His work in you. Thank the Father for the gift of the Holy Spirit, who enables you to abide in the love and the obedience of the Lord Jesus. Believe firmly that the triune God works in your heart and has His hidden "heaven" there, which will be revealed to you as your heart is wholly given to His Son and Spirit. "Through [Christ] we . . . have access by one Spirit to the Father" (Eph. 2:18).

Learn this important lesson: The stronger your faith in Christ the more freely will the Spirit flow from you. The more you believe in the ever-abiding Spirit the more surely you will know that Christ dwells and works within.

The Spirit and Christ

He will glorify Me, for He will take of what is Mine and declare it to you.

John 16:14

WE have seen that Christ spoke of the gift of the Spirit as the fruit of faith in Christ. The Spirit would "flow as a river" from those who believed in Christ (see John 7:38). Today we have the other side of this truth: the Spirit also flows from Christ. We thus see that the Spirit both reveals Christ and imparts Him. This is a lesson of deep importance.

Do you desire the Spirit? Have faith in Christ who bestows His Spirit. Do you desire Christ? Rely upon the Spirit to reveal Christ to you. The Spirit is sent from Christ (who is now glorified in heaven) to impart this glorified Christ to us upon earth—so that Christ may be glorified in our hearts.

We have seen that the fullness of the Godhead dwelt in Christ in order that Christ, as the life of God, might dwell in us. All the life and love of God which the Spirit imparts to us is in *Christ*. Our *whole life* now consists of being in union with Christ. As the branch is in the vine, so are we in Christ and He in us. Our first requirement each new day, then, is to acknowledge that Christ lives in us and that the Holy Spirit will make this an abiding reality. *Count upon the quiet, unseen working of the Holy Spirit in your heart.*

Oh Christian, this truth, so deep and so divine, is almost beyond our finite grasp. The Spirit of the Holy One, who is God, will reveal it to us. Cling in childlike trust to Christ, confident that the Holy Spirit is working silently within you so that Christ may dwell in your heart by faith. Make it a matter of prayer every day that "[the Father] would grant you" *that day* "to be strengthened with might by his Spirit in the inner man; that Christ may dwell in your hearts by faith" (Eph 3:16–17). *Fix* your heart upon Christ on the cross and upon Christ on the throne in childlike trust. While you do so, Christ will be revealed in your heart by the Holy Spirit and you may confidently say: Christ lives in me—Christ is my life!

Carnal or Spiritual?

And I, brethren, could not speak to you as to spiritual people
but as to carnal, as to babes in Christ.

First Corinthians 3:1

THE difference St. Paul makes between the two kinds of Christians is of great importance. Man's natural life is altogether carnal. The Christian at his new birth receives the Holy Spirit, and immediately there begins a struggle between the flesh and the Spirit. So long as the Christian allows the Spirit to conquer, and is led by the Spirit, the power of the Spirit over him increases, and he becomes a spiritual man. The flesh, however, is still there, and in the flesh is no good thing. But the Christian then learns that his flesh was crucified with Christ—as something that deserves the accursed death—and he becomes a spiritual man of whom it may be said: "The spiritual man makes judgment about all things" (see 1 Cor. 2:15).

When, on the other hand, the Christian is ignorant about the Spirit—or, if informed, disobedient—then the flesh obtains the mastery, and the Christian remains weak; and as there is no spiritual growth, he remains a babe. He may try in his own strength to do better, and what was begun in the Spirit is continued in the flesh—a carnal attempt to become holy (see Gal. 3:3). By degrees the flesh triumphs, so that he has no power to resist the works of the flesh or the spirit of the world.

This is the sad, sad condition of the church, that the majority of her members remain carnal. They constantly fall under the power of the flesh and, as a result, are overcome by envy and anger and uncharitableness. Such Christians have no insight into spiritual truth. If their life in Christ is mentioned, or daily fellowship with Him, or what God promises to do for His children, they can hardly understand what is meant.

How earnestly we should each pray God to reveal to us what is carnal and what spiritual, and to enable us to yield ourselves completely to the guidance of His Spirit.

Go On to Perfection

But solid food belongs to those who are of full age.

Hebrews 5:14

Therefore, leaving the discussion of the elementary principles of Christ, let us go on to perfection.

Hebrews 6:1

IN the epistle from which this text is taken we read that the Hebrews had long been Christians and now ought to be teaching others, but instead they were still like babes needing to be fed on milk (see 5:12–14). The apostle seeks to rouse them by "leaving the discussion of the elementary principles of Christ . . . not laying again the foundation of repentance" (6:1). They were to go on to perfection, to the status of full-grown men, and be prepared for deeper truths which would be taught to them regarding Christ as the High Priest. "But He, because He continues forever, has an unchangeable priesthood. Therefore He is also able to save to the uttermost those who come to God through Him, since He always lives to make intercession for them" (7:24–25).

The truth of this ever-abiding unchangeable priesthood and complete salvation is the solid food of the believer who desires maturity. In chapter 9 we are told of Christ appearing before the face of God for us and, later, that we may now enter into the holy place to live in communion with God (see 10:19–20). It is only when the Christian ceases to speak of the first principles of Christ, not laying again a foundation of repentance, that he will grow and be strengthened in grace. He will then actually live in full fellowship with Christ.

Oh Christian, if hitherto you have been content to know that you have repented and trusted in God, and so are sure of salvation, I beseech you, do remember that this is only the foundation and beginning of eternal life. Listen to the call to press on to perfection. This is what God desires and what the Son Himself will do for you. Learn to yield yourself fully to Christ and to find daily in Him the hidden life of the spirit, so that you may grow in grace and God can use you as a soul-winner. Nothing less than this conformity to Jesus Christ should satisfy you—a life wholly dedicated to God and to His dear Son.

The Building and Its Foundation

*Let us go on to perfection, not laying again the foundation of
repentance from dead works and of faith toward God.*

Hebrews 6:1

JESUS' parable about the difference between founda-
tions and their effect on the houses built on them
should teach us important lessons about the two kinds of
life. St. Paul has laid for us the foundation of the house of
God: the doctrine of justification by faith in Jesus Christ.
That truth is the one sure, immovable fact upon which a
lost sinner grounds his eternal salvation (see Rom. 5:2).

What is the house built upon this foundation? Read
Romans 5:9–18. There the apostle points out that justification and peace with God are not everything—they
are only the beginning. Then he goes on to show that
as in Adam we died, so in the second Adam (Christ)
we receive the abundance of grace whereby we may live
through Jesus Christ. This is the life which is built on the
unshakable foundation. He points out in Romans 6 how
in Christ we have died unto sin and are baptized into
His death. And as we are united to Him in His death, we
also share in His resurrection—an entirely new life. If we
have died with Christ, we may be sure we really are dead
to sin but alive unto God in Jesus our Lord.

It is our union with the crucified and risen Christ
that sets us free from the power of sin; and through the
Spirit Christ Jesus releases us *wholly* from the dominion

of sin. This life in Christ is the edifice that must be built upon the foundation of justification.

How little is the truth of Romans 6 grasped or appropriated! We are ever ready to lay again the foundation and be content with that. No, child of God, our experience must be deeper! We must realize that Christ is our life that we are crucified with Him and in Him, and in Him we are both dead and risen again. Only that truth will enable us to live a holy, godly life in the joy of the Holy Spirit.

The Reformation

But let each one take heed how he builds on it. For no other foundation can anyone lay than that which is laid, which is Jesus Christ.

First Corinthians 3:10–11

"NO other foundation"—these words to the Hebrews are certainly not applicable to the Reformation period. In the course of many centuries the church of Rome had left the true foundation and built on another. Instead of justification by faith in Jesus Christ being the foundation of the Christian life, the church itself claimed power to forgive sins. Forgiveness could be obtained only through a priest; indeed, it might be bought from a priest for money. The great work of Luther and Calvin was to lay anew the foundation of Jesus Christ, to the comfort of thousands of anxious souls. We can never thank God enough for the Reformation, when Jesus was proclaimed anew as our righteousness—our peace with God.

That great work of reformation was not accomplished in a day or a year. It took fifty years to establish the Reformation, and even after that time there were many former priests whose conversion experience did not include the power of living a holy life. Calvin himself said the Reformation was more in doctrine than in the changed lives of the people, and he felt deeply the need for the people to be taught and trained in the paths of righteousness. It is no wonder that, because the foundation had first to be relaid in the full truth of conversion and faith, there was a delay in the building of a proper and adequate structure on that true foundation—the building, that is, of a life of sanctification.

The Reformation is sometimes thought of as a return to Pentecost, but it was by no means that. Instead of a flourishing of brotherly love, increased separation from the world and an earnestness in preaching Christ by all who loved Him, there arose much controversy among the Reformers. They trusted too much in the patronage of statesmen who were kindly disposed towards them, and preaching was seen as the work of ordained ministers only. This is much in contrast to the Pentecostal witnessing for Christ by all those who were constrained by His love.

The Reformation was certainly necessary—a start in the right direction. But in many ways it was far from adequate. Therefore, "let us go on to perfection" (Heb. 6:1).

The Walk in Christ

As you therefore have received Christ Jesus the Lord, so walk in Him, rooted and built up in Him and established in the faith, as you have been taught, abounding in it with thanksgiving.

Colossians 2:6–7

HERE again we have the two kinds of life. The first is described in the words, "You have received Christ Jesus." That includes conversion, forgiveness of sin through the blood of Jesus Christ, and acceptance as a child of God. Then comes the second, the walk in Christ, "rooted in Him," as a tree that must each moment receive its life from the earth in order to bear fruit. "Built up in Him," who is the only foundation. "Established in the faith . . . abounding in it with thanksgiving," by which each day the Christian by his walk and conversation proves that he abides and lives in Christ. As the roots of a tree receive life uninterruptedly from the soil, so the Christian receives his life and power moment by moment from abiding in Christ.

In the confessions of faith drawn up by the Reformers, prominence is given to conversion, acceptance of Christ. *Justification* and *justified* are words in frequent use. But the word *sanctification* is rarely found. Emphasis is laid on the doctrine of the forgiveness of sin, of faith in Christ as our righteousness before God, but we find little about Christ living in us and our life being rooted in Him. The Heidelberg Catechism gives an explanation of the Ten Commandments, but Christ's commands in Matthew 5 and John 13–16 are hardly mentioned.

Let us thank God for the Reformation as a time when the foundation truth of a crucified and fully sufficient Savior was laid. But at the same time let us go on to perfection, to a daily uninterrupted walk in Christ wherein we may abound in faith, experiencing the abundance of grace from the fullness there is in Christ for us to enjoy daily. The earliest description of true godliness is in the words: "Enoch walked with God" (Gen. 5:22). So Christians must learn to walk in Christ daily, established in the faith and abounding in it.

The Mediator of a New Covenant

You have come . . . to Jesus the Mediator of the new covenant, and to the blood of sprinkling.

Hebrews 12:22, 24

A MEDIATOR is responsible to see that both sides shall faithfully fulfill their obligations as set forth in any covenant. Jesus is declared to be our mediator: He is our surety that God will fulfill His promise. He is also surety to God for us that we on our part shall faithfully perform what God requires of us. In other words, He will *enable* us to keep the covenant.

It was as Mediator, on the night of the Last Supper, that He gave His disciples the great promise of a new covenant, the gift of the Holy Spirit as prophesied by Ezekiel.

He also undertook to fulfill the promise, "I will . . . cause you to walk in My statutes, and you will keep My judgments and do them" (Ezek. 36:27). It was in fulfillment of this promise that He spoke so definitely to His disciples about the keeping of His commandments being the way by which God's designs would be accomplished. "If you love Me, keep My commandments. And I will pray the Father, *and He will give you another Helper*" (John 14:15–16); "He who has My commandments and keeps them, it is he who loves Me. And he who loves Me will be loved by My Father, *and I will . . . manifest Myself to him*" (14:21); "If anyone loves Me, he will keep My word;

and My Father will love him, *and We will come to him and make Our home with him*" (John 14:23); "If . . . My words abide in you, you will ask what you desire, *and it shall be done*" (15:7); "If you keep My commandments, you will abide in My love" (15:10); "You are My friends if you do whatever I command you" (15:14).

Would the Lord categorically have said that all these blessings depend upon the keeping of His commandments if it were impossible for His disciples to keep them? Assuredly not. He had given them a pledge that the Holy Spirit would enable them. Meditate on this until you have the assurance that Christ expects His disciples, out of love for Him, through the power of the Holy Spirit to do all that He asks. It is through the Spirit's abiding in their hearts that they will unceasingly keep His commands.

Better Promises

*[He is] Mediator of a better covenant, which was
established on better promises.*

Hebrews 8:6

*You have come . . . to Jesus the Mediator of the new
covenant, and to the blood of sprinkling.*

Hebrews 12:24

WE have here some of the better promises of the
new covenant. Jeremiah 31:33: "This is the covenant . . . I will put My law in their minds, and write it
on their hearts"; Jeremiah 32:40: "I will put My fear in
their hearts so that they will not depart from Me"; Ezekiel
36:25–27: "I will cleanse you from all your filthiness.
. . . I will give you a new heart and . . . I will put My
Spirit within you and cause you to walk in My statutes,
and you will keep My judgments and do them"; Ezekiel
36:36–37: "'I, the LORD, have spoken it, and I will do
it.' Thus says the Lord GOD: 'I will also let the house of
Israel inquire of Me to do this for them.'"

Could there be better or more definite promises
than these, that God Himself would put His fear into
the hearts of His people so absolutely that they would
not depart from Him, and that He would cause them to
keep His judgments and do them?

This is the new covenant of which Jesus is Mediator. Through the Holy Spirit He dwells in us and will
keep us from sin, so that we shall have the desire and the

power to do God's will in all things. Think of Zacharias' inspired words as he prophesied the deliverance Christ would bring. Luke 1:74–75: "That we, being delivered from the hand of our enemies, might serve Him without fear, in holiness and righteousness before Him all the days of our life." These are the words of God and show what He will do for those who inquire of Him. The promises are sure. The Mediator gave first His *blood* and then His *Spirit*. He sees to it that the better promises are fulfilled to those who wholeheartedly and confidently desire and claim them from Him. Alas, how seldom is such a life either preached or experienced!

Fellowship with God

That which we have seen and heard we declare to you, that you also may have fellowship with us; and truly our fellowship is with the Father and with His Son Jesus Christ.

First John 1:3

F*ELLOWSHIP with God is the unique blessing of the gospel.* Christ died for us "that He might bring us to God" (1 Pet. 3:18)—that the prodigal son might return to the father's house and to a life in his father's love. By His blood Christ dedicated for us a new and living way into the holy place where we may walk in the light of God. The promise is, "They walk, O Lord, in the light of Your countenance. In Your name they rejoice all day long" (Ps. 89:15–16). Our walk with God may be as natural and as joyful as a walk in the sunshine. A life of unbroken fellowship with God—this is the gospel.

Fellowship with God is the preacher's theme. If preachers are content to speak only of conversion, forgiveness of sin, and safety after death, they will fail grievously in their work. Christians must be educated to practice the presence of God—to have fellowship with God, thereby ensuring holy living. This was the apostle John's message: fellowship with the Father and with His Son Jesus Christ.

Fellowship with God is the preacher's only source of power. If fellowship with God is the blessing of the gospel and the burden of the minister's preaching, then it follows that the preacher must show in his own life the possibility and blessing of such a walk with God. Experiencing it himself, he is able to tell others of it as being most blessed and full of joy. A life of close fellowship with the Father and with the Son lived by the preacher gives him the right to win others to the same joyous fellowship. "What God can do for me, He can do for you." May fellowship with the Father and with His Son Jesus Christ be our daily life: first in the quiet hour, then in our daily duties, and finally in winning souls for Christ that they, too, may share this full salvation.

The Fullness of Christ

And the Word became flesh and dwelt among us, and we beheld His glory, the glory as of the only begotten of the Father, full of grace and truth. . . . And of His fullness we have all received, and grace for grace.

John 1:14, 16

READ these words again and again until you come under the impression of the supreme fullness of Christ. Let the Holy Spirit teach you to worship this Christ as the One in whom dwells all the fullness of the Godhead.

I may receive a purse containing very little or nothing at all, or the purse may contain many gold coins. There is a great difference between the two! And so with us as Christians. Some receive Christ with the forgiveness of sin and the hope of heaven but know little of the fullness of Christ and all the treasure there is in Him. Other Christians are not satisfied and sacrifice all things until they can say, "Of His fullness we have all received, and grace for grace." St. Paul said: "I also count all things loss for the excellence of the knowledge of Christ Jesus my Lord" (Phil. 3:8). Like the merchant seeking goodly pearls who, when he had found the pearl of great price, sold all that he had in order to buy it (see Matt. 13:45–46), so is the Christian who grasps something of the fullness of Christ: His outflow of love and joy, His holiness and obedience, His utter devotion to the Father and to mankind. That Christian gives up all so that he may be *united* to this Christ. Listen to our Lord's words: "These things I have spoken to you, that My joy may remain in you, and that your joy may be full" (John 15:11); "Your heart will rejoice, and your JOY no one will take from you" (16:22); "Ask, and you will receive, that your joy may be full" (16:24).

Dear reader, do you know this Christ in whom all fullness dwells? Or do you live as a pauper, depending largely upon the world for joy? It is God's will that Christ should fill all things, even your heart and its needs. Let the Holy Spirit imprint deeply upon your heart the words of our text in all its fullness.

The Heavenly Life

*You died, and your life is hidden with Christ in God.
[Christ] is our life.*

Colossians 3:3–4

IT is of the utmost importance for a Christian to know
that the new life which he receives actually is the life
of Christ which He lives in the Father. Our life, my life,
is hid with Christ in God, and must daily be received
anew and preserved as a holy of holies.

It takes time and quiet thought and prayer to in any
measure grasp this great marvel—that the life Christ lives
in the Father is the same life He lives in me. Christ does
not live one life in the Father and another in me. His
words are: "Because I live, you will live also. At that day
you will know that I am in My Father, and you in Me,
and I in you" (John 14:19–20). As He is in the Father,
so are we in Him and He in us. One divine life is in the
Father and in Christ and in me.

How little have we grasped this! How little trouble
do we take to experience it! Here is the secret of the neces-
sity of taking quiet time and prayerful meditation each
day to become deeply impressed with the glorious truth
that the Lord Jesus, whose life is hid in God, has also His
life hid in me. It is only by taking time to realize that the
heavenly Christ *lives in my heart* that I shall truly live as a
child of my heavenly Father. When we allow God's Holy
Spirit *daily* to renew in us that heavenly life in Christ,

then we shall grasp what it means to say "I died with Christ" and "I die daily to sin and self and the world in order to make room for the increase of the life that Christ actually lives in me." Then we shall experience that "our citizenship is in heaven" (Phil. 3:20). Thus shall I have courage to believe that Christ lives in me and reigns and works that which is well-pleasing to His Father. Thus shall my life be a humble and constant walk with God, in the fellowship of His holiness and His love.

A Royal Priesthood

You are a chosen generation, a royal priesthood.

First Peter 2:9

IN the Old Testament, the thought of the kingdom took first place; in the New Testament, prominence is given to the topic of priesthood.

One of the chief reasons for the feeble life in the church today is the mistaken idea that the main object of God's grace is man's happiness. A fatal error! God's aim is far holier and far higher. He saves men for the purpose that they in turn shall carry out *His* purpose, which is the saving of their fellow men. Each believer is appointed to be the means of imparting to others the new life he has received.

Those who are saved have the holy calling of being channels of God's grace to others. The feeble state of the church is largely due to the fact that most Christians imagine that their chief concern is to desire and receive sufficient grace to reach heaven after death. The church must so proclaim the gospel that each saved soul shall, rather, apprehend this message: "You have been saved to serve—saved to save others."

"You are . . . a royal priesthood." A royal priesthood! The priestly heart is above all things a sympathetic heart in which the love of Christ constrains us to win souls for Him. And that comes by virtue of two compelling motives: love to Christ, whom I shall please and honor in winning others to love Him; and love for souls, which will constrain me to sacrifice everything so that others may share this heavenly life.

A priestly heart! A heart that has access to God in prayer and intercession for those who are yet unconverted! A priestly heart that, having pleaded in prayer for souls, has courage to speak to them of Christ! A priestly heart, in which the life of Jesus, the Great High Priest who ever lives to make intercession, is continued, and His power to save to the uttermost is manifested! Oh Spirit of God, write upon my heart, with indelible letters, "A royal priesthood."

Apart from Me—Nothing

*He who abides in Me, and I in him, bears much fruit; for
without Me you can do nothing.*

John 15:5

THE Lord Jesus follows up His great promise that
those who abide in Him will bear much fruit with
the words, "Without Me you can do nothing."

What a cause for humiliation! This is because the nature we inherit from Adam is so corrupt that in us—that
is, in our flesh—dwells no good thing. Nay, more, our
flesh is at *enmity* against God. We are under the power of
sin to such an extent that we are unable to do anything
well-pleasing to God.

What a call to repentance! How often we as Christians have thought that we were able to do that which is
good. How often we thought we were making ourselves
better. Let us remember Christ's words, "Without Me you
can do nothing," and henceforth rely only upon Him.

What cause for thanksgiving! Christ has united us to
Himself, and so dwells within us. He may work in and
through us each day and all day. This is the secret of the
spiritual life: the Lord Jesus working in us, enabling us
to do His work.

What cause for joy and encouragement! All that in
the Christian life has appeared too high and unattainable
for me, all that will *Christ* work in me. I have to care for
one thing only—that I remain utterly dependent upon

Him to care for me and work through me all the day. Whenever I remember "Without Me you can do nothing," I remember, too, "He who abides in Me . . . bears much fruit."

He Himself will see to it that He abides in me, and He challenges me to abide in Him. This dependence on Him—a constant dependence—is, praise God, the great work of which the eternal Spirit will make me capable. Thank God for the life of Christ in me. "I in Him, He in me" is the work of the Holy Spirit in each soul that humbly and believingly yields itself for such communion with God.

Day 21

The Thrice-Holy God

*The God of peace Himself sanctify you completely; and may
your whole spirit, soul, and body be preserved blameless at
the coming of our Lord Jesus Christ. He who calls you is
faithful, who also will do it.*

First Thessalonians 5:23–24

WHAT inexhaustible words! The God of peace
Himself. Yes, He Himself, and none other, can
and will do the work. And what is this work? To sanctify
you wholly. How is this work to be done? Your entire
spirit and soul, and even your body, is to be preserved
without blame at the coming of our Lord.

This promise is so great it appears incredible. The
apostle feels the difficulty and adds the words, "He who
calls you is faithful, who also will do it." That leaves no
room for doubt but calls us to place our confidence in
the faithfulness of God.

This work is accomplished by the Holy Trinity. God
the Father says, "Be holy, for I am holy" (Lev. 11:45).
"I am the Lord who sanctifies you" (Exod. 31:13). The
Son prayed, "For their sakes I sanctify Myself, that they
also may be sanctified by the truth" (John 17:19). And
the Holy Spirit is the Spirit of sanctification, through
whom the church of God consists of the sanctified ones
in Christ Jesus (see 1 Cor. 1:2).

How does the thrice-holy God accomplish this great
work of sanctifying us wholly? Through His continual

indwelling and fellowship and the breathing of His holy life into us. As upon a cold day a man may warm himself by standing in the rays of the sun until its warmth penetrates his body, so the soul who takes time for communion with God becomes permeated with the strength of the triune Holiness.

Oh, my brother, what a treasure there is in these words, what cause for adoration, what confidence that God, who is faithful, will do it. What encouragement to wait upon Him—to walk with Him, as Abraham did, knowing God, being fully assured that what He had promised He was able to perform. God grant us a vision of this divine holiness and grace and power, that we may confidently feel that He will sanctify us wholly and preserve spirit, soul, and body without blame.

The Spirit of His Son

Because you are sons, God has sent forth the Spirit of His Son
into your hearts, crying out, "Abba, Father!"

Galatians 4:6

THE Spirit that dwells in you, Oh child of God, is no less than the same Spirit that was in Christ, the Spirit of God's holiness. In Gethsemane He taught Christ to cry, "Abba, Father, Your will be done." He teaches us to know God's father-love and to respond with childlike love and obedience. He will be in us even as He was in Christ, the Spirit of Sonship expressing Himself in a life of prayer. I may most assuredly expect of Him that He will impart to me God's love and holiness.

I may also rely upon Him as the Spirit of God's Son to reveal Christ in my heart and always to keep alive in me Christ's life. All that Christ has said of His abiding in me and I in Him, the Spirit of Christ will work in me. Through the Spirit, Christ's indwelling becomes an actual experience, and as a result the mind of Christ and His disposition may be formed in me and become manifest. I may with certainty expect this of the Holy Spirit.

And furthermore, the Holy Spirit will fit me for God's service. As the Spirit that sanctifies, He will reveal Christ to me as my *sanctification*. The Spirit will enable me to overcome the world and its entanglements and be a witness to what Christ's life in His child may be. He will fill me with love to the brethren, with love to those who hate or ignore me, with love to all around me who are not yet saved, so that I might pray for them and be ready to help them. He will give me a love reaching to all the world so that I may labor with enthusiasm for missions, that the gospel may be taken to all men.

Oh my brother, take time each day with the Lord for your heart to be filled with the confident expectation of what God's Spirit will do for you.

You Were Bought at a Price

Do you not know that your body is the temple of the Holy
Spirit who is in you, whom you have from God, and you
are not your own? For you were bought at a price; therefore
glorify God in your body.

First Corinthians 6:19–20

HERE you have a reply to the question: What does the Spirit expect of me? Your body is His temple. The temple of God is holy, devoted to His service. You are not your own, you have no right to please yourself. You have been dearly bought with the blood of Christ. The Spirit has absolute right to your whole life. Therefore you must glorify God in your body and your spirit, which are God's. The Holy Spirit is the Spirit of God's holiness; He comes to make me holy. He expects me to obey Him fully.

Let me dwell upon these words that I may comprehend clearly what the relationship must be between the Spirit and me, and what it is He has a right to expect of me. He asks that I, *as one dearly bought with the blood of Christ, and no longer my own*, shall seek in all things to *please Him* and to *follow His leading*. All that I owe to God, and to the Lord Jesus, must be shown in my conduct towards the Holy Spirit. I must in all things be guided by Him, for as God He has absolute right to me. He expects me to say each morning, "'Speak, LORD, for Your servant hears' (1 Sam. 3:9). I yield myself to obey the prompting of Your voice within me." He expects absolute obedience.

Furthermore, He expects that I shall keep in close touch with Him by taking time each day to renew the bond between Him and me. My whole life must be yielded to Him that He may bring to perfection in me all His glorious fruits.

He also expects that in His strength I shall witness for Jesus Christ and consider it my work to help to bring the souls around me to the Lord Jesus. The Spirit expects that my body, which has been dearly bought, shall be a temple of God from which adoration and praise to God the Father and His Son Jesus Christ shall continually arise.

Revival

Restore us, O God; cause Your face to shine, and we shall be saved!

Psalm 80:3

Restore us, O God of hosts; cause Your face to shine, and we shall be saved!

Psalm 80:7

Restore us, O LORD God of hosts; cause Your face to shine, and we shall be saved!

Psalm 80:19

ISRAEL was in sore need. Their enemies scoffed at them as if God had forsaken them. Three times the psalmist uses the words of our text to reinforce his prayer: "Stir up Your strength, and come and save us!" (80:2)

In our day the Enemy rejoices that, in spite of our many churches, Christianity is so powerless in overcoming the sins of drunkenness, immorality, worldly-mindedness, and love of money. God's children are asking: "Can nothing be done? Is there no hope of revival?" Is God not willing to lead His people into a fuller, deeper life of victory over sin and all that opposes Christ in Christian and heathen lands? Has not God in His great love promised to give us His Spirit in answer to prayer? Is God not waiting for our prayers to begin the work of revival? A revival is much needed, and it is possible. God is longing for us to claim His promise and exercise our right as members of the royal priesthood (see 1 Pet. 2:9).

Where must the revival begin? With God's children, who may offer themselves to God as instruments to be used by the Holy Spirit, separating themselves from sin and devoting themselves to the work of saving souls. Christians must realize and prove that the object of their life is God's service and the saving of those for whom Christ shed His blood.

Revival has already begun wherever God's children offer up everything to live and work and suffer as Christ did.

Dear child of God, it avails little to desire a deeper or more abundant life unless this is the chief object: to be a witness for Jesus and to win others to His service, and to intercede for them as a labor of love.

A Threefold Cord

Whatever things you ask when you pray, believe that you receive them, and you will have them.

Mark 11:24

TO *know, to feel, to will*: These are the three chief activities of the soul. When a Christian realizes the fullness there is in Christ and the abundant life He gives, then these three words will show him the way to participate in this fullness.

To know. We must not be content with our own thoughts about growth in grace. We must see to it that we know clearly *what God promises to do in us*, and *what He requires of us*. God's Word teaches us that if we come honestly, with all our sin and impotence, and sincerely yield to Christ our Lord, He will do in us far above what we dare think. See to it that you know clearly what God says you may ask of Him.

To feel. We must be careful to desire with our whole heart that for which we pray, and be willing to pay the price for it. It may be our desire is faint. God will create the proper appetite in answer to prayer. It may cost us a struggle, and much self-sacrifice, to let go of the world and self, but the Spirit will come to our aid. But without strong desire and self-sacrifice, progress will not be made.

To will. The will is the most important point: only by firmness will faith have courage to appropriate what God bestows. Often in the midst of fear and struggle, and almost in despair, we *will* to grasp what God offers. Our confidence must be in God alone. Christ Jesus will give us the assurance that He is strengthening us to yield ourselves to the Spirit's guidance. When our desire has developed into a firm will, we shall have courage to believe all that God has promised.

Child of God, thousands have by these means come to experience such fullness in Christ as they never thought possible. The more you cast yourself upon the Word of God and the love and power of Christ, the sooner will you enter into the rest of faith that ceases from works and depends upon God to fulfill His purposes in you.

The Vine and the Branches

He who abides in Me, and I in him, bears much fruit.
John 15:5

IN this parable we see what the new life is which the Lord promised His disciples would be the work of the Holy Spirit. It clearly mirrors the life of faith.

1. "Does not bear fruit," "much fruit," fruit that remains (see 15:2, 8, 16): The one object of the life of faith is to bear much fruit to the glory of God the Father.

2. Cleansing (see 15:2): the indispensable cleansing through the Word that is sharper than a two-edged sword.

3. "Abide in Me" (15:4): intimate, continuous fellowship.

4. "I in you" (15:4): divine indwelling through the Spirit.

5. "Without Me you can do nothing" (15:5): complete impotence, deep humility, constant dependence.

6. "My words abide in you," "If you keep My commandments, you will abide in My love," "You are My friends if you do whatever I command you" (15:7, 10, 14): indispensable obedience.

7. "[If] My words abide in you, you will ask what you desire" (15:7): limitless confidence of faith.

8. "It shall be done for you" (15:7): powerful answer to prayer.

9. "As the Father loved Me, I also have loved you; abide in My love" (15:9): life through faith in Him that loved me.

10. "These things I have spoken to you, that My joy may remain in you, and that your joy may be full" (15:11): joy full and abiding.

11. "This is My commandment, that you love one another as I have loved you" (15:12): the new commandment kept through the power of Christ's love in our hearts.

12. "[I] appointed you . . . that your fruit should remain, that whatever you ask the Father in My name He may give you" (15:16): the all-prevailing name of Christ.

This is the life Christ makes possible for us and works in us through the Holy Spirit. This is the life so sadly wanting in the church and yet so indispensable. This is the life assured to childlike faith and obedience.

Give Time to God

To everything there is a season, a time for every purpose under heaven.

Ecclesiastes 3:1

THIS is literally true, there is a time for everything. Can it be true, as so many maintain, that there is no time for communion with God? Is not the most important matter for which we must find time *fellowship with God*, in which we may experience His love and His power? *Give God time*, I beseech you.

You need time to feed upon the Word of God and to draw from it life for your soul. Through His Word, His thoughts and His grace enter our hearts and lives. Take time each day to read the Bible, even if it be only a few verses; meditate upon what you have read, and thus assimilate the bread of life. If you do not take the trouble to let God speak to you through His Word, how can you expect to be led by the Spirit? Meditate upon the Word, and lay it before God in prayer as the pledge of what He will do for you. The Word gives you matter for prayer, and courage and power in prayer. Our prayers are often futile because we speak our own thoughts and have not taken time to hear what God has to say. Let the Word of God teach you *what God promises, what you need, and in what manner God wishes you to pray.* Thus by prayer and the Word your heart will be prepared to have fellowship with God through faith in Christ Jesus.

Dear child of God, it is of little use to speak of the deeper, more abundant life of Christ as our life if we do not daily, above all things, take time for communion with our Father in heaven. The life and love and holiness of God cannot be ours amidst the distractions and temptations of the world unless we give God time to reveal Himself to us and to take possession of our hearts.

Deeper Life

Some fell on stony places, where they did not have much earth; and they immediately sprang up because they had no depth of earth.

Matthew 13:5

THE seed sown upon the rocky places where the soil was superficial sprang up quickly, but it withered as quickly because there was no depth of earth. We have here a striking picture of so much religion which begins well but which does not endure. The Christian needs a *deeper* life. Let your whole life be an entrance into that love which surpasses knowledge. In Ephesians 3:17–19, St. Paul prays "that Christ may dwell in your hearts through faith; that you, being rooted and grounded in love, may be able to comprehend with all the saints what is the width and length and depth and height—to know the love of Christ which passes knowledge; that you may be filled with all the fullness of God." He prays that Christians may stand rooted, first, in the love of Christ which surpasses knowledge, realizing and acknowledging that the depth of this love reaches beyond knowledge. He believes it possible for the soul of a Christian to be so rooted in this love that he may be filled with the fullness of God to the greatest extent that may be granted to a saint while upon earth.

And how may we attain to this? "I bow my knees to the Father" (Eph. 3:14). The way to remain rooted in love begins in humble prayer upon your knees before God. Furthermore, "that He would grant you, according to the riches of His glory"—great indeed, and wonderful—"to be strengthened with might through His Spirit in the inner man" (Eph. 3:16). There must be inner strengthening by the Spirit. Only in the life that knows the powerful working of the Spirit is such a life rooted in love possible. And yet more, "that Christ may dwell in your hearts through faith" (3:17). The most important requirement is that Christ in His everlasting love shall dwell in you every day, ensuring a life ever more deeply rooted in the love of Him who gave Himself for us.

I beseech you, dear child of God, take time to bow before the Lord in prayer, and thus meditate upon and appropriate these words. Do not begrudge time or trouble. Commune with the Christ who loved you with the same love with which the Father loved Him, so that you may get an insight into the greatness of the condescension of that love to you.

Soul-Winning

He who abides in Me, and I in him, bears much fruit; for without Me you can do nothing. . . . By this My Father is glorified, that you bear much fruit.

John 15:5, 8

FRUIT is that which a tree or a vine yields for the benefit of its owner. Hence, all that the Lord Jesus has taught us about His abiding in us and we in Him is to make us understand that this is not for our benefit but for His good pleasure and the honor of the Father. We as branches of the heavenly Vine receive and enjoy this astounding grace so that we may win souls for Him.

May not this be the reason why you have not enjoyed unbroken fellowship with Christ? You have forgotten that the object of fellowship and communion is fruit-bearing in saving others. Have you not given too much thought to your own sanctification and joy, not remembering that as Christ sought His blessing and glory from the Father in the sacrifice of Himself for us, so we too are called to live solely to bring Christ to others? It is for this purpose that we become branches of the heavenly Vine—in order to continue the work that He began, and with the same wholeheartedness.

When Christ was on earth He said, "I am the light of the world" (John 9:5); but speaking of the time when He would be taken from the earth He said, "You are the light of the world" (Matt. 5:14).

How often you have said to the Lord, "I yield myself to You for cleansing and keeping and to be made holy," but you have hesitated to add "to be used of You for the salvation of others." Let us acknowledge our failure here and humbly offer ourselves to the Lord for His work. Let us begin by praying for those around us, seeking opportunities of helping them and not being satisfied until we bear fruit to the glory of the Father.

Christ said, "Without Me you can do nothing." He knows our utter weakness. He has promised, "He who abides in Me . . . bears much fruit." Let all that we learn of the more abundant life and God's abounding grace constrain us to live to win souls for Jesus.

Intercession

*If anyone sees his brother sinning . . . he will ask, and [God]
will give him life.*

First John 5:16

IN that last night, when the Lord Jesus promised to
send the Holy Spirit to His disciples, He said: "At
that day you will know that I am in My Father, and you
in Me, and I in you"; "Abide in Me, and I in you"; "He
who abides in Me, and I in him, bears much fruit" (John
14:20; 15:4, 5). This was a new relationship, and the fruit
thereof would be attained by prayer. They would pray
and He would grant their desires.

He made a sevenfold promise: "Whatever you ask in
My name, that I will do" (14:13). "If you ask anything
in My name, I will do it" (14:14). "[If] My words abide
in you, you will ask what you desire, and it shall be done
for you" (15:7).

"[I] appointed you . . . that whatever you ask the
Father in My name He may give you" (15:16). "Whatever
you ask the Father in My name He will give you" (16:23).
"Ask, and you will receive, that your joy may be full"
(16:24). "In that day you will ask in My name" (16:26).

Read the above seven texts over and over until you
are convinced that the believer who abides in Christ
has the right to pray for souls, and that Christ and the
Father will answer his prayer. Remember, too, that you
are a branch of the heavenly Vine not only for your

own salvation but that you may bear much fruit in the conversion of souls. It is as an intercessor that grace is granted you to pray for others, believing assuredly that God will answer you.

Think of the change that would come over a community if every believer in it would take time to pray for those who do not believe. How God would be glorified in our bearing much fruit! Dear child of God, take time to allow God to write these glorious promises upon your heart.

Christ Our Life

You died, and your life is hidden with Christ in God. . . .
[Christ] is our life.

Colossians 3:3–4

LET us now sum up what has been said about the new life we are to live in Christ. Let us see if we have grasped the lesson this booklet would teach us, and whether we really intend to live this life.

St. Paul writes to the Colossians: "You died, and your life is hidden with Christ in God." Only God's Spirit can enable the believer to grasp and appropriate the truth that he was actually crucified and died with Christ. The new life he receives in Christ through the Spirit is life out of death—resurrection life! Christ reigns now as the Lamb in the midst of the throne, and the power of that life is shown as a crucified life in each one who has received it. The Holy Spirit gives me the assurance that I died with Christ, and the power of His death and resurrection works in me.

Look once again at these words: "Your life is hidden with Christ in God." This fully agrees with what Christ said on the last night: "You will know that I am in My Father, and you in Me" (John 14:20)—my life is with Him in the Father. My life is safely hid with Christ in God, and from there I each day by faith receive it anew through the working of the Holy Spirit.

But is this truth generally believed and proclaimed? Sadly, no. Is this not the reason why so many of God's children make so little progress? They do not know that the life of Christ who died on the cross and now lives in heaven is truly *their* life hidden in God and is to be daily received afresh from God in the quiet hour. What joy to know my spiritual life is not in my keeping, but is hidden in God. Christ and the Holy Spirit will grant to each humble, believing child of God a personal appropriation of this new life.

What joy to know that the new life of God's children around me is also hidden with Christ in God! What a bond of unity this will be. How sincerely we should love each other and pray for each other.

"Your life is hidden with Christ in God. . . . [Christ] is our life."

Oh Spirit of God, let me rely upon You to make this true in my life!

Fort Washington, PA 19034

This book is published by CLC Publications, an outreach of CLC
Ministries International. The purpose of CLC is to make evangelical
Christian literature available to all nations so that people may come
to faith and maturity in the Lord Jesus Christ. We hope this book has
been life changing and has enriched your walk with God through the
work of the Holy Spirit. If you would like to know more about CLC,
we invite you to visit our website:

www.clcusa.org

To know more about the remarkable story of the founding of
CLC International we encourage you to read

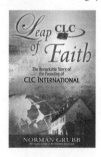

LEAP OF FAITH

Norman Grubb

Paperback
Size 5¹/₄ x 8, Pages 248
ISBN: 978-0-87508-650-7
ISBN (e-book): 978-1-61958-055-8

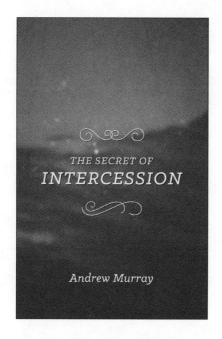

THE SECRET OF INTERCESSION

Andrew Murray

The Secret Series books contain a wealth of teaching that is based on Andrew Murray's mature and full experience in Christ. *The Secret of Intercession* contains one month of daily selections that reveal the power of intercession.

Paperback
Size 4^1/$_4$ x 7, Pages 67
ISBN: 978-1-61958-249-1
ISBN (*e-book*): 978-1-61958-250-7

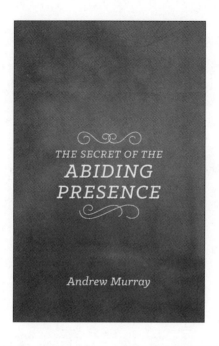

THE SECRET OF THE ABIDING PRESENCE

Andrew Murray

The Secret Series books contain a wealth of teaching that is based on Andrew Murray's mature and full experience in Christ. *The Secret of the Abiding Presence* contains one month of daily selections that reveal the peace that comes with resting in the presence of God.

Paperback
Size 4¹/₄ x 7, Pages 67
ISBN: 978-1-61958-251-4
ISBN (*e-book*): 978-1-61958-252-1

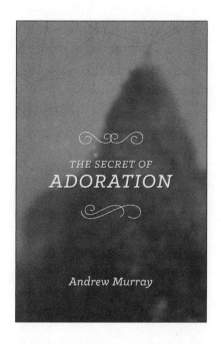

THE SECRET OF ADORATION

Andrew Murray

The Secret Series books contain a wealth of teaching that is based on Andrew Murray's mature and full experience in Christ. *The Secret of Adoration* contains one month of daily selections that highlight the importance of true worship in the lives of believers.

Paperback
Size 4¹/₄ x 7, Pages 71
ISBN: 978-1-61958-253-8
ISBN (*e-book*): 978-1-61958-254-5

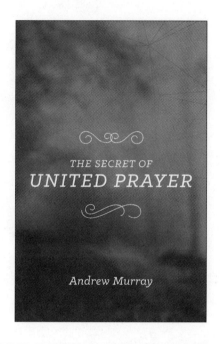

THE SECRET OF UNITED PRAYER

Andrew Murray

Part of the classic *Secret Series*, *The Secret of United Prayer* contains one month of daily selections on the power of united prayer. Murray expresses his desire that many would join the ranks of intercessors—those who pray continually, in unison, for the church of Christ and His kingdom on earth. He studies the "lost" secret of Pentecost: the sure promise that the power of the Holy Spirit will be given in answer to fervent prayer.

Paperback
Size 4^1/$_4$ x 7, Pages 67
ISBN: 978-1-61958-272-9
ISBN (*e-book*): 978-1-61958-273-6